ANIMAL ABILITIES

OCTOPUSES

Anna Claybourne

Chicago, Illinois

To contact Capstone Global Library, please call 800-747-4992, or visit our web site www.capstonepub.com

Edited by Laura Knowles, Abby Colich, and Diyan Leake
Designed by Victoria Allen
Original illustrations © Capstone Global Library Ltd 2013
Illustrated by HL Studios
Picture research by Elizabeth Alexander
Originated by Capstone Global Library Ltd
Printed and bound in China by CTPS

17 16 15 14 13
10 9 8 7 6 5 4 3 2 1

Library of Congress Cataloging-in-Publication Data
Claybourne, Anna.
   Octopuses. -- (Animal abilities)
Cataloging-in-Publication data is available at the Library of Congress.

ISBN (PB): 978 1 4109 5247 9
ISBN (HB): 978 1 4109 5240 0

Acknowledgments
We would like to thank the following for permission to reproduce photographs: Alamy p. 25 (© Jeff Rotman); Corbis pp. 14 (© Stringer/New Zealand/X01244/Reuters), 22 (© Bettmann), 28 (© Will Gray/JAI), 29 (© Melvin G. Tarpley/US Army/Handout/Reuters); © Kaylene Kau www.coroflot.com/kaylene p. 26; The Maritime Aquarium at Norwalk (CT, USA) p. 21; Nature Picture Library pp. 7 (© David Shale), 8 (© Jeff Rotman), 9 (© Jeff Rotman), 12 (© Jose B. Ruiz), 15 (© Nature Production), 17 (© Constantinos Petrinos); Photoshot pp. 13 (David Fleetham), 20 (Picture Alliance/Jens Büttner); Shutterstock pp. 4 (© Rich Carey), 6 (© Bjorn Stefanson), 11 (© Mike Bauer), 18 (© EcoPrint), 23 (© bluehand), 24 (© Boris Pamikov); Superstock p. 19 (© Masa Ushioda/age footstock); Tamar Gutnick p. 16; Visuals Unlimited, Inc. p. 27 (Massimo Brega/The Lighthouse). Design feature of an octopus silhoutte reproduced with permission of Shutterstock (© Potapov Alexander).

Cover photograph of a coconut shell octopus reproduced with permission of Corbis (© Hal Beral).

Every effort has been made to contact copyright holders of material reproduced in this book. Any omissions will be rectified in subsequent printings if notice is given to the publisher.

Contents

Some words are shown in bold, **like this**. You can find out what they mean by looking in the glossary.

Meet the Octopus

Even if you have never met an octopus, you will know one when you see one! There is nothing else quite like this slippery sea creature.

Arms or legs?

The word *octopus* means "eight feet"—but octopuses do not have feet! They have eight long, slithery arms that can crawl, stretch, and curl around objects. The arms are often called legs or **tentacles**. However, true tentacles, which **squid** have, are longer and thinner than octopus arms.

There are around 300 octopus **species**. This one is called a big red.

Squishy but smart

Octopuses are **invertebrates**, which means they do not have backbones. They have no skeletons at all—just soft, squishy bodies. They are part of a group of animals called **mollusks** and are related to slugs, snails, and clams.

Invertebrates often seem like pretty simple creatures. But octopuses (along with their close relatives, squid and cuttlefish) have some amazing skills and abilities and behave in all kinds of clever ways.

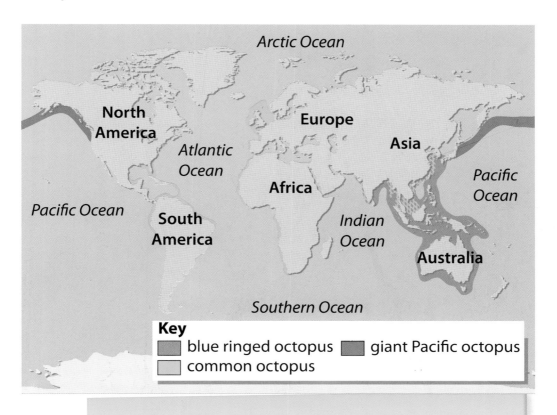

Octopuses live almost everywhere in the oceans, from rock pools and reefs to the deep seabed. This map shows where some of the octopuses you will find out about in this book live.

Being an Octopus

Many octopuses are **nocturnal**. They rest during the day and come out at night to hunt **prey** such as crabs and clams. Octopuses can crawl along on the seabed using their arms or swim along in the water.

Living alone

Most octopuses live alone. They like feeling enclosed, so they make a cozy den in a pile of rocks, in a gap in coral, or even in an old oil barrel. They rest and eat their food in the den.

This big red octopus is taking shelter in coral.

AT RISK?

No octopuses have been listed as **endangered**, because not enough is known about them yet. However, experts think some types could be at risk of dying out.

Octopus sizes

The common octopus has a body as big as a soccer ball, with arms up to 3 feet (1 meter) long. Other octopuses range from small enough to sit in your hand to ocean giants with arms that are 13 feet (4 meters) long.

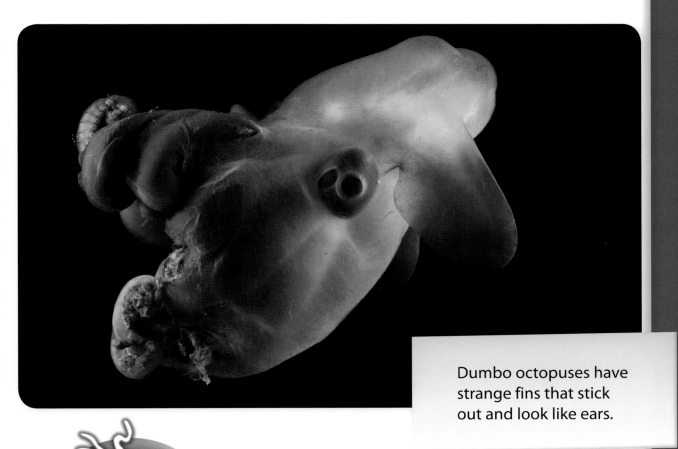

Dumbo octopuses have strange fins that stick out and look like ears.

HOW DO WE KNOW?

Since humans cannot breathe underwater, studying sea creatures can be tricky. Scientists go diving or snorkeling to watch octopuses in the wild. They also study **captive** octopuses in aquariums and science labs.

Octopus Bodies

In cartoons, octopuses are often shown with a large, oval head on top of their eight arms. In fact, this is the octopus's sack-shaped body, or mantle. Its head is between its body and its arms, with the hard mouth, or **beak**, in the middle. Since octopuses have no bones or joints, the eight arms are packed with muscles that can make them curl, twist, and turn in all directions.

OCTOPUS INK

When in danger, an octopus can squirt thick, black ink out of its siphon to confuse attackers.

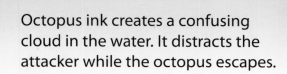

Octopus ink creates a confusing cloud in the water. It distracts the attacker while the octopus escapes.

Body parts

In this picture, you can see all the most important parts of an octopus's body.

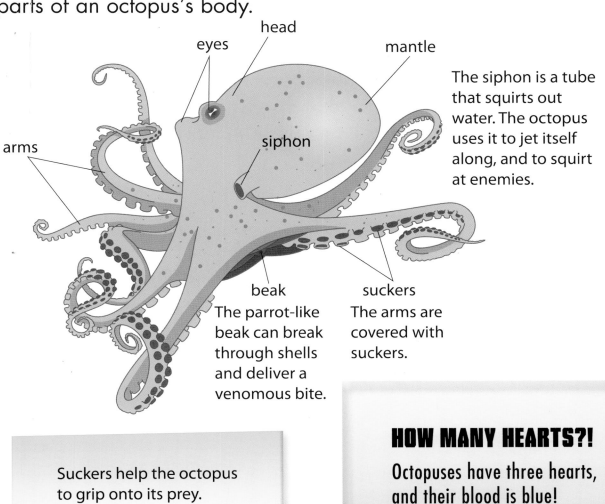

eyes

head

mantle

The siphon is a tube that squirts out water. The octopus uses it to jet itself along, and to squirt at enemies.

arms

siphon

beak
The parrot-like beak can break through shells and deliver a venomous bite.

suckers
The arms are covered with suckers.

Suckers help the octopus to grip onto its prey.

HOW MANY HEARTS?!

Octopuses have three hearts, and their blood is blue!

Octopus Brains and Senses

Scientists have found that octopuses actually have nine brains! Besides the main brain in the head, each octopus arm has its own "mini-brain." These mini-brains are long bundles of nerves that deal with all the arms' movements and sensations, as this would be too much for a single brain to manage.

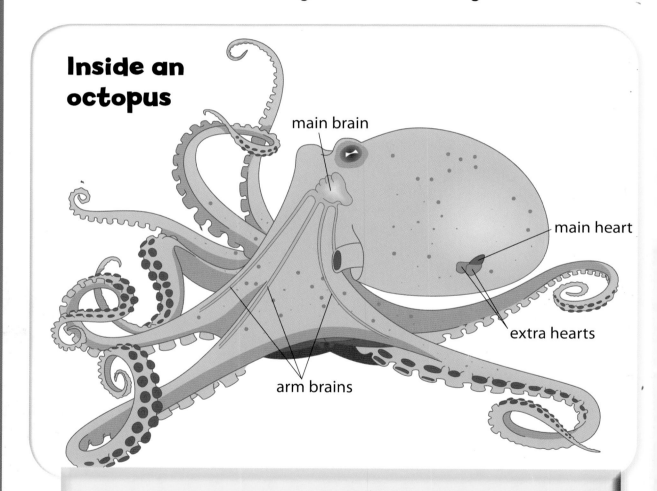

Inside an octopus

main brain

main heart

extra hearts

arm brains

BIG BRAINS

Octopuses have large brains for their body size, which could partly explain why they are so smart. Other animals that have big brains for their body size include tree shrews, humans, chimpanzees, dolphins, and crows.

Super-sensors

Octopus arms and suckers are amazingly sensitive. An octopus feels around with them, poking into narrow cracks in search of prey. In addition to having an amazing sense of touch, the suckers can taste and smell, too. Octopuses use them to check whether what they are touching is good to eat and to sense smells and tastes floating in the water.

Octopuses also have very good eyesight. They have no ears, but they can hear a little by using other body parts to sense the ripples made by sounds.

Octopuses have large eyes with slit-shaped pupils.

In Disguise

Octopuses are masters of **camouflage** and disguise. Chameleons are famous for changing color, but an octopus can do it much better and much faster. Even more amazing, octopuses can also change their shape and texture.

For example, an octopus can make itself look just like a clump of frilly seaweed or a bumpy rock, then transform back into a smooth, rounded octopus shape again. Or it can flash a series of bright colors across its skin.

This common octopus is matching its body to the surrounding rocks and seaweed.

The mimic octopus can disguise itself as other animals. This one is pretending to be a dangerous sea snake.

How do they do it?

Camouflage tricks help octopuses to confuse and startle **predators**, hide for safety, or sneak up on their prey.

An octopus's skin is covered in tiny color spots called chromatophores, surrounded by muscles. The muscles control each spot, to make it much bigger or make it disappear. This lets an octopus create all kinds of different patterns on its skin. It can also tighten muscles under its skin to change its shape and create a bumpy surface texture.

A TIGHT SQUEEZE!

An octopus can make its body so narrow that it can squeeze through a hole almost as small as its own eyeball.

Learning

Some animal abilities, such as the way a spider spins a web, are instincts. This means they are built into an animal's brain and happen automatically. But most animals can learn things, too.

Experiments have shown that octopuses are great learners. They can learn to recognize different shapes or to get a snack out of a maze. They can even learn to do a task, such as opening a box, by copying another octopus.

This captive octopus named Octi has unscrewed a plastic bottle to reach a snack.

How and why?

Most intelligent animals, such as humans, chimps, and dolphins, live in groups and learn from their families as they grow up. Octopuses are different. Most species only live for a year or two. Also, octopus parents die when their eggs hatch and do not teach their babies anything. Then why are they so good at learning? Scientists are still not sure.

After they hatch, baby octopuses must fend for themselves.

HOW DO WE KNOW?

An Italian scientist named Graziano Fiorito is famous for his octopus experiments. In one test, an octopus managed to open a screw-top jar after seeing another octopus do it first. It seemed to learn the trick just by watching.

Solving Problems

When faced with a problem, octopuses will keep trying to figure it out. They can find their way through mazes, figure out how to reach a hidden treat, or search for an escape route from a tank. And if they succeed, they will remember the solution for the next time.

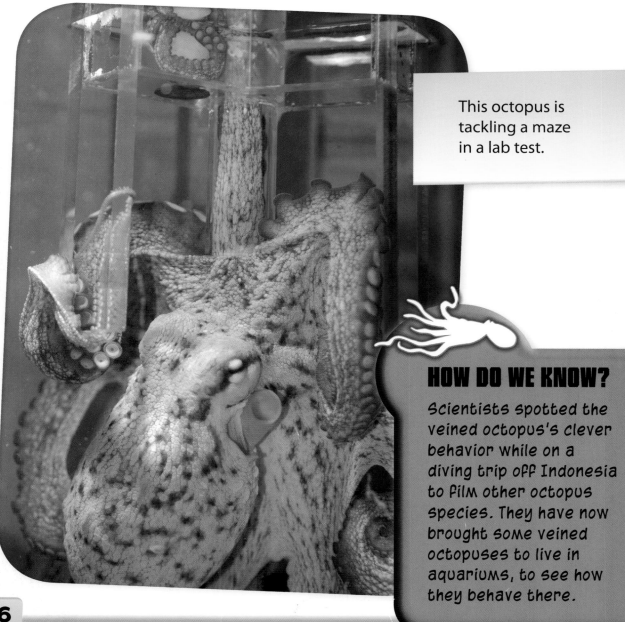

This octopus is tackling a maze in a lab test.

HOW DO WE KNOW?

Scientists spotted the veined octopus's clever behavior while on a diving trip off Indonesia to film other octopus species. They have now brought some veined octopuses to live in aquariums, to see how they behave there.

A better way

Like other intelligent animals, octopuses often find new ways to do things. In the wild, they collect stones or shells to make doors for their dens. Some use their siphons as cleaning jets to blow their food leftovers, such as broken seashells, out of their dens.

The veined octopus of southeast Asia carries seashells or coconut shells around with it and uses them to hide inside. To do this, the octopus must be smart enough to plan ahead and think about how things could be used. Scientists think the veined octopus is one of the few invertebrates known to use tools.

A veined octopus walks on tiptoe, carrying useful shells under its body.

Sneaky Tricks

A famous octopus story dates from the 1870s, when workers at an aquarium in England were puzzled to find that fish were missing. One morning, an octopus was found with the fish. It had been sneaking out of its own tank in the night, stealing fish to eat, then going home again!

Octopuses can survive for a while in the open air. This is why they sometimes go exploring out of their tanks.

Octopuses are great escape artists. Scientists and aquarium workers find them on the floor, hiding in drains, or even crawling up shelves. They are strong and can push up tank lids and pull out plugs, in addition to wriggling through tiny cracks.

Out of the water!

Octopuses breathe underwater, but as long as their bodies are wet, they can survive in the air for a while. In the wild, they sometimes scramble over rocks and seaweed between rock pools. They can also escape from fish markets and try to slither away on the sidewalk.

ARMLESS OCTOPUS

The banded drop-arm octopus can shed an arm on purpose as a way to avoid being eaten. The arm wriggles around to distract the predator while the octopus escapes. The octopus can then regrow the arm. This regrowing is called regeneration.

This octopus has lost two of its arms, but they are growing back again.

Having Fun

Do octopuses play? It can be hard to tell, but some do appear to enjoy themselves!

Playing alone

Many animals like playing together. Since octopuses live alone in the wild, they do not do this. However, it is possible to play on your own, and some experts believe many octopuses like playing with toys.

This octopus in an aquarium appears to be interacting with the visitors.

PET OCTOPUSES

Having a pet octopus might sound like fun, but it is not a good idea unless you are an expert. Octopuses need special salt water and lots of cleaning and feeding—and they do not live for very long.

In one test, scientists gave captive octopuses empty pill bottles. They all handled the bottles for a while, but two played games with them. One kept blowing hers into the water current, then waiting for it to "bounce" back like a ball.

Look at me!

In aquariums, octopuses sometimes seem to dance around and get excited when visitors are there. They may follow people back and forth or even show off a series of shape and color changes. Keepers and owners also say octopuses can recognize people they know.

Workers give toys to octopuses in aquariums so they can use the skills they would use in the wild. This may stop them from getting bored.

21

Humans and Octopuses

Humans have a long history with octopuses. For centuries, we mainly just wanted to catch them and eat them! In the past, we used octopus ink for writing. More recently, we have begun to keep octopuses in aquariums and as pets. Scientists have been able to learn much more about them.

Old legends tell of octopus-like sea monsters dragging down ships. However, no known octopus is big enough to do this.

These octopuses are for sale at a fish market in Japan.

メキシコ産
K 1.400.—

モワッコ産 (中)
K 2.000.—

What does an octopus taste like?

People usually describe octopus meat as smooth, chewy, and slightly fishy-tasting. It is a healthy food and is very popular in Italy, Spain, Portugal, Japan, and Korea. However, some people think it is not right to eat such an intelligent animal.

PAUL, THE WORLD CUP OCTOPUS

In 2010, a common octopus living at a Sea Life Center in Germany predicted the winners of eight World Cup soccer matches in a row, including the final. He picked his favorites by choosing from two food boxes marked with the playing teams' national flags. No one knows how he decided!

Octopus Science

To do experiments on octopuses, scientists usually catch them from the wild. They also design their experiments carefully, to suit octopus abilities.

This scientist is photographing a giant Pacific octopus in the wild.

Getting it right

In experiments with octopuses, mazes, puzzles, and toys have to work well underwater. Octopuses must be kept in separate tanks, or they might eat each other. If a maze leads to a tasty crab or mussel reward, all the equipment must be clean, with no fishy scent trails. Otherwise, the octopus might simply be following the smell rather than figuring out the maze.

Personality test

In the 1990s, scientists tested 44 red octopuses to see if they had different personalities. They wrote down how each octopus behaved when it was approached, touched with a brush, and fed over a two-week period. Some octopuses were much bolder, more active, or more sensitive, while others were more relaxed or shy.

OCTOPUS CHEMICALS

In addition to octopus behavior, scientists study octopuses' muscles and brains and the chemicals in their bodies. Studies of octopus bite **venom** have found they contain chemicals that could make medicines for treating allergies or cancer.

This giant Pacific octopus is being tagged so that scientists can track its movements at sea.

Copying the Octopus

Octopuses and their amazing abilities have inspired some super-cool inventions, both old and new.

Sticky suckers

Have you noticed rubber or plastic suction cups on bathtub mats, toys, and other objects? They were developed in the 1860s and were based on the shape of octopus suckers. Large suction cups are used to carry sheets of glass, and people have even used specially designed rubber suction cups to climb skyscrapers!

PART OCTOPUS

One inventor has designed a wriggly **prosthetic** octopus arm that can be attached to a human arm. It shows how this type of robot could help people who have lost limbs.

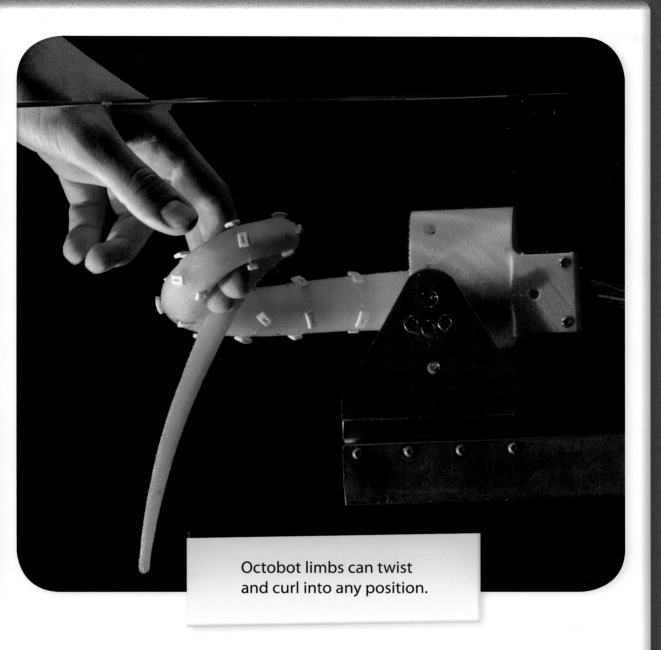

Octobot limbs can twist and curl into any position.

Octobots!

Some scientists are making a new type of robot that copies the way octopuses move their arms. Most robots have hard, fixed limbs that work like our bones and muscles. "Octobot" limbs are flexible. In the future, octobots could be used to carry out underwater rescues.

The Amazing Octopus

There are a lot of amazing animals out there, but octopuses really are extraordinary. Their shape-shifting and color-changing abilities, disappearing acts, and clever tricks make them seem almost alien. Yet we used to think of these creatures as pretty simple—boneless, blob-like, and tasty to eat. As scientists keep studying octopuses, imagine what else they could discover!

Climbing is much harder work for us than it is for an octopus.

Octopus superpowers

Since you are human, you are already intelligent and good at learning and problem-solving. But what if you could have any of the octopus's amazing abilities?

- If you had eight arms covered with suckers, they would be useful for multitasking, and your super-sucker grip would be great for sports and climbing.

- If you had shape-shifting abilities, you could squeeze through tiny gaps, create all sorts of crazy costumes, or turn your body into an umbrella on a rainy day.

- If you had color-changing skills, you could blend into the background so that no one could see you!

- If you had a water siphon for jetting along, you would zoom through the pool and break every swimming record.

- If you could squirt ink, you could splatter anyone who bothered you and maybe invent a new way of painting, too!

Since we do not have color-changing skills, we have to wear special outfits when we want to camouflage ourselves.

Glossary

beak octopus's hard, biting mouth, shaped a bit like a parrot's beak

camouflage colors and patterns that blend in with the background or surroundings

captive held in a zoo, aquarium, or laboratory instead of living in the wild

endangered at risk of dying out

invertebrate animal without a backbone

mollusk animal without a backbone, with a soft body and a shell; part of the group that includes slugs, snails, and mussels

nocturnal active at night

predator animal that hunts and eats other animals

prey animal that is eaten by other animals

prosthetic human-made body part, made to replace a part that is missing

species particular type of living thing

squid type of animal related to the octopus. Squid have a long head rather than a rounded one and eight arms and two tentacles.

tentacle long, thin body part, often with a paddle-shaped section at the end, found in squid, but not octopuses

venom poison from a bite or sting

Find Out More

Books

Spilsbury, Louise. *Octopus* (A Day in the Life: Sea Animals). Chicago: Heinemann Library, 2011.

Wallace, Karen. *Gentle Giant Octopus* (Read, Listen, and Wonder). Cambridge, Mass.: Candlewick, 2008.

Web sites

animal.discovery.com/invertebrates/octopus
The Animal Planet web site features videos, puzzles, and more about octopuses. Scroll down to find lots of links.

kids.nationalgeographic.com/kids/animals/creaturefeature/octopuses
Find lots of information about octopuses on the National Geographic web site.

nationalzoo.si.edu/animals/invertebrates/facts/cephalopods/factsheets/pacificoctopus.cfm
The National Zoo web site includes lots of facts about the giant Pacific octopus.

Places to visit

There are lots of aquariums with live octopuses. Try these:

John G. Shedd Aquarium,1200 S. Lake Shore Drive, Chicago, Illinois 60605
www.sheddaquarium.org

Monterey Bay Aquarium, 886 Cannery Row, Monterey, California 93940
www.montereybayaquarium.org

Index